There Was A Time

Selected Poems
by William Gelish

Cover photo *Dix Hills Sunset* by William Gelish

Special thanks to Andy McLaughlin
for making the dream of creating this book a reality

Dedicated to the memory of
Joseph and Helen Gelish
My true heroes

Part I   There Was A Time

There Was a Time   15
Dazed and Confused   17
Listen to the Wind   19
There Will Be   21
Another Life   23
Small Dose   25
I Died   27
The Poet's Soul   29
Michael   31
The Bridge   33
Pay As You Go   35
The Image of Myself   37
Anne Marie   39
When I Used to Love You   41
One Side   43
Embracing the Pain   45
When I Sing and Play Guitar   47
The Sweetest Place (Ever)   49
My First Time   51
I Live With It   53

Part II   Love's Surrender

I Wonder What   57
A Certain Way   59
It's All Good   61
I Remember   63
Lost Love   65
If Only You   67
Come to Me   69
A Long Time Ago   71
The Gift   75
If I Had a Christmas Wish   77
Undying Love   79
How Quickly You Forget   81
One Petal at a Time   83
Night Song   85
No One Will Ever Know   87
Bon Voyage   89
Why I Love July   91
My Dreams Are Still of You   93
The Muse   95
A Different Kind of Love   99
I Thought About You   101
Fall From The Sky   103
Indifferent Homicide   105
The Color Blue   107
Love's Surrender   109

Part III   The Gypsy

Sorrowful Living   113
Dark Thoughts (A Vampire's Prayer)   115
The Poet's Words   117
In The Shadows   119
I Have Grown to Love You   121
For What of This Curse?   123
The Party   127
Cruisin'   129
The Gypsy   131
The Truth About The Truth   133
Rendezvous   135
Alone   137
Elegance   139
In Despair   141
Love and Hate   143
Living The Dream   145
The Legend of Don José   147
Fright Night   149
Outside   151
The King of West Babylon   153
This Dream Called Life   155
The Secret of The Blind Man   157
The Circle   159

Part IV   Awaken My Heart

This Feeling   163
Ruthie   165
Let Me Try   167
Personal Poetry   169
Goodbye Misery   171
Daddy's Songs   173
My Perfect Night   175
Beyond Belief   177
I Try   179
Wedding Song   181
The Jewel   183
Inner Demon   185
Cry   187
While She Lays Sleeping   189
Vision of Summer   191
My Forever Love   193
The Breakdown   195
Make Me Understand   197
Awaken, My Heart   199
O Passionate Love   203
The Eroticism of Death   205

Part V The Countdown

A Tale of Woe 209
The Countdown 211
It Comes Back to You 213
Desolation of the Soul 215
Cause For Alarm 217
Depression 219
Symbolism 221
The Words of the Dead 223
Time Ticks Away 225
What Finer Fate Than Death 227
Unfinished 229
The Last Day of the Year 231
Going to the Graveyard 233
Regrets 235
If I Die Tonight 237
The Invisible 239
I Don't Know Why 241
It Takes a Long Time 243
I Become Like Starlight 245
The Day You Left 247

Part I

There Was a Time

There Was a Time

There was a time
When I was young
I thought I'd never die

But then I found
My only love
With time for just good-bye

They say there's some
Who never love
There is no doubt about it

That love alone
Is here to stay
There is no doubt about it

There was a time
That I could feel
The music in my soul

But now it's late
My mind won't wait
It's only Rock and Roll

They say there's some
Who die so young
They blow their brains away

And others live
Another life
That makes them want to stay

There was a time
I didn't see
What life was all about

But I could see
What I would be
I never had a doubt

They say there's some
Who's gonna change
And others never will

There's some I'll never
See again
And yet I love them still

Dazed and Confused

Travel back in time with me
A puff of smoke is all you'll see
Everybody's hair was long
Nothing happened that was wrong

Partying our lives away
All night long, into the day
Music blasting in the car
Never traveled very far

Didn't know we had it all
We were back in school by Fall
All this time, so long ago
How we got by, I don't know

Hung out with my friends all night
We were higher than a kite
Rock and Roll was all we knew
Did just what I wanted to

We got naked at our school
Sure knew how to play the fool
All the girls I loved before
They don't love me any more

Tried my best to be a star
Didn't get me very far
Had a car and drove around
My feet never touched the ground

Four years on the mountain top
I could party till I'd drop
Stumbled through my life, I guess
It was fun, I must confess

Listen to the Wind

Listen to the wind
And it will tell you
All you need to know
About life
It can take you
Anywhere you want
To go
And back again
And it will remind you
Of everything
That was or ever will be
But be careful
You may enjoy the ride
Too much
And be sorry when it's gone
And sad
Try not to remember
It's invisible power
To go anywhere
Any time
You cannot possess it
And it will not stay
More than a little while

There Will Be

My heart has awakened
Like the fog off the rolling sea
And the new trees on the forest floor
There will be no thing like beginning

It was a long long sleep
A dream that transcends reality
And the dreamer longs to continue after awakening
There will be no dream like this one

And long ago, but not too far away
The song once sang so sweetly
Is hummed again in someone's head
There will be no song so beautiful

When the night is darkest
And the minutes seem like years until dawn
The soul lives only with hope
There will be no day like yesterday

But life was meant to live
And no one guaranteed
That we would have more than yesterday
There will be no idea like tomorrow

Another Life

Another life
A different wife
It all is done
Where has it gone
I tried to hide
My other side
At night I'd park
Where it was dark

And drove around
Without a sound
This all is true
What made me blue
I had to cry
In days gone by
Wanted it all
My mind was small

Just used my tongue
When I was young
It all was easy
My life was breezy
And played the game
I'm not the same
I was so high
Barely got by

Thought I was rich
Ain't life a bitch
I took a fall
Then had to crawl
When I was done
It wasn't fun
To be alone
No one to phone

I cried and cried
Thought I had died
It took me years
And lots of tears
I finally found
What goes around
Comes back to you
That much is true

So I began
To have a plan
That I'd get through
What I had to
And do my best
To never rest
Until I find
Some piece of mind

And so today
I've found my way
Now I get by
Because I try
Don't need a drink
To help me think
I use my brain
It keeps me sane

I now deplore
Those days before
But won't let hate
Become my fate
Another life
A different wife
It all is done
Where has it gone

Small Dose

Love, I've had a small dose
The eyes have it
I can't wait until tomorrow
I just need a small dose

Evening, as I've known it before
The sun follows me to my bed
And I don't dream at night

Tortured, the soul of a man in
a desparate situation
He looks anywhere for love
And denies himself his past

Small dose, just wanted someone
to share my fantasy
That two people can be together
As one

I died

I died
But I lived
It's okay

I saw
I believed
It's real

I loved
And I lost
It's hard

I thought
That I knew
It's crazy

I sweat
And I bleed
It's a shame

I've longed for
And I've wanted
It's a game

I was complete
I was a man
It's all gone

I'm all right
I go on
It's called Life

The Poet's Soul

Something fills the poet's soul
So he has the desire to share it with
the world
If only they could know:
How he's loved and lived and
suffered, truly suffered
For the poet's soul is filled to
the limit
With love and passion
And with death and hate
He lives with his burden
Restrained inside him
If only he could write it down
And share it with the world
But he plants a seed
And wants a tree to grow
It may take a lifetime
As he travels the road of life
He is truly alone with his thoughts
He only shares them in the late
hours of the night
And he cannot sleep because his
soul does not rest
I often wonder
How many of these souls
Still roam the Earth after their
bodies are gone
They continue their lonely journey
If they could only find the light
They were born in a hurricane
And they died in the darkness
It is only their poems
That illuminate their existance
As the souls that they were
The poet's soul

Michael

We thought about you yesterday
The first day you were gone
There were still some things left to do
That never would be done
As long as we remember you
And since you were a boy
All I can say for everyone
Is that you brought us joy

But life is short, we never know
Just when our time is through
We never knew how very short
Our time would be with you
So now our lives will just go on
As we remember you
We never will forget the days
And good times spent with you

And yet we must continue on
Without being too sad
For we remember all the love
And spirit that you had
Then with God now, forever more
We pray you'll always be
And Michael we'll remember you
With love for all to see

The Bridge

There is a bridge
That once crossed
From which we
May never return
Life has many paths
The road goes on
Every day is different
But when we choose
Which way to go
We must decide
Whether or not
To cross over
And change our lives
With such uncertainty
Of our destination
That we may become
Strangers to ourselves
The way that we have lived
And all that we are

Pay as You Go

As I go forward
To and fro
I guess we all
Pay as we go
That one decision
For the best
Has consequences
For the rest

You can pay later
Or pay now
I guess it's all
The same somehow
It's one step forward
Two steps back
Enough to cause
A heart attack

Sometimes a price
That we don't see
I know that's how
It has to be
And if you think
There's a free ride
Then you'd be wrong
You'll soon decide

I live to fight
Another day
But soon will find
The price I'll pay
And to get even
Would feel good
To feel the way
I wish I could

I'll be content
With what I know
And end up where
I want to go
But everything
It has it's cost
Sometimes it's only
Time we've lost

Still, saving for
A rainy day
Won't help you to
Be on your way
Or move you forward
To and fro
I guess we all
Pay as we go

The Image of Myself

The image of myself:

... lonely
Repelled by others whose lives have
taken an unwavering course

... careless
Without concern for people with
or without whom, my life will continue
to be my own

...free
From those things that could
destroy my desire and spirit

... anxious
For what the future may
bring

... loving
Those people who continue to
bless my soul

... lost
But with the definite feeling that
I'm headed in the right direction

... cold
As I feel the winds of change
blowing around my every step

... tired
Yet ignoring the weariness
and continuing on

Anne Marie

Oh Anne Marie, sweet Anne Marie
You are the star of all my dreams
From many years ago, my dear
A different world, or so it seems

And for the first time I did hear
The quiet beating of my heart
Especially when you did sing
I knew you tore my world apart

And now it seems, we've been as one
For oh so very many years
You never have deserted me
When I did cry my lonely tears

I love you more than you will know
Your songs have always rescued me
And helped me try to figure out
How sweet that life and love can be

When I Used to Love You

When I used to love you
A long time ago
There was nothing to stop me
As if I didn't know

And when I was twenty
It just was us two
I wasn't quite sure
That I knew what to do

Now I have all the answers
To those questions then
And if you would ask me
I would do it again

For the days without wisdom
Are the finest, you see
When you're not really sure
What you're going to be

Now I am so tired
But I can't go to sleep
I've so many promises
I have to keep

But tonight I remember
When my love, it was true
I remember those days
When I used to love you

One Side

There's only one side to life, can't you see
That it's not about you, it's just all about me

And doing what's right, well it's just fine, I guess
But how do I get myself out of this mess?

I try to see things the way that others do
It's just that they never seem to follow through

The mistakes that they make are just too big to miss
But I don't see my own, when I'm acting like this

And they miss the big picture, again and again
Only I see things clear, with a magical zen

Don't they know that I'm right, all the time, don't they see
That they'd be better off, if they listened to me

When I drive down the road and see others drive by
I know they could improve, if they only would try

And I try and I try to make everything right
Then I wonder why everyone else wants to fight

So I get on my high horse and think I'm so cool
And I wonder why everyone else is a fool

Sometimes I can't sleep, with the way things are now
I'm just hoping I'll straighten it all out, somehow

And if they could all come to my side, they would see
That it's not about them, it's just all about me

Embracing the Pain

Breathe it all in and feel it
You have just begun to live
Having never before felt the pain
You are only just alive

If you are awake every day
Your memory can provide you
With all the reality you need
And the fantasy that you crave

But the nights are sleepless
As you journey in your mind
You lie awake all night
Awake and aware of everything

Take care that this reality
Does not take more than it gives
For you will find yourself, one day
Enjoying it all and embracing the pain

When I Sing and Play Guitar

When I sing and play guitar
I feel like a Superstar
You can tell, I know my part
Every single word by heart
It goes deep into my soul
Feel like I could lose control
Rockin', Rollin' really loud
Jimi Hendrix would be proud

Sing my heart in every word
Saddest songs you ever heard
Sometimes love songs, sometimes Rock
I can play around the clock
Just as each new day goes by
You don't need a reason why
Pick up your guitar and play
We feel different every day

You can play just what you feel
Songs are best when they are real
I sang my heart out tonight
Music is my heart's delight
When you hear it loud and clear
You may even shed a tear
A broken heart, a lover's song
It's how you feel, it's never wrong

Just leave it there for all to hear
Emotions that you hold so dear
It feels just like a friend you tell
When things go bad or when they're well
There are no secrets you can't share
And you can tell them, if you dare
To say just why you have the blues
Because you had to pay your dues

To sing of love above them all
Considering the rise and fall
When love is ended and you're sad
Remembering the things you had
Fantasy, or what is real
It all comes down to how you feel
Telling things the way they are
When I sing and play guitar

The Sweetest Place (Ever)

Can you come with me
On this journey
Across time and space
Unto an existence
When everything I knew
Went in slow motion

I never wanted it
To have an ending
But, as you know
Nothing ever
Stays as it is
Or can be as it was

And so I journey
Inside my mind
To find where I left you
In a perfect dream
And when I wake up
I can hardly remember

What is reality
And what I have imagined
For all my traveling
The sweetest place ever
Is the one that
Never existed at all

My First Time

It was the best
With someone who
I loved so much
When it was through
I pledged my heart
Forever more
Like nothing else
Ever before
The music played
And "Let it be"
Became the words
For her and me

I drank some beer
Met her outside
The high school dance
We would decide
That in the woods
Over the hill
Is where we both
Would get our thrill
It wouldn't last
For very long
When we were done
It felt so wrong

I Live With It

I live with it
Horrible and ugly
Grotesque and deformed
Staring back at me
Never striving for greatness
The truth being inconvenient

I play at it
Feeding the poor and hungry
Helping those less fortunate
Showing great empathy
Compassion poorly feigned
Existing for one purpose

It must be fed
Addicted only to myself
Pleasure and pain intertwined
Something new, always the same
Adding to some collection
Never get quite enough

It is eternal
The Harvest of seeds sown
Self indulgent suicide
The Burning of the Saints
Losing all spiritual comfort
The adulation of myself

Part II

Love's Surrender

I Wonder What

I follow my journey backwards
To the place where I began
I'm intoxicated by the feeling
I wonder what you're doing
    Tonight

And everything is nothing
What I believed, wasn't to be
And I'm filled with confusion
I wonder what you did
    Yesterday

But I continue to believe
Because I know no other way
I cannot change who I am
I wonder what you'll do
    Tomorrow

So I wait and I wonder
If anything ever happened at all
Or was it just a dream
I wonder what you might do
    Someday

A Certain Way

There's a certain way I feel
It's different every day
And yet somehow, it stays the same
In some uncertain way

I know that feeling will be there
And last me for some time
I'm not afraid that it will end
Some day you will be mine

And as the time goes by, I know
Although it seems so strange
It's just like it was long go
Somehow it cannot change

For love, it lasts eternal
With style and with such grace
I feel it deep inside my bones
As clearly as your face

And even though it's been so long
And that you might forget
I'm hoping you'll remember soon
I haven't finished yet

Some guys will give you flowers
And take you out at night
But I'm the one who's always there
I'll always treat you right

So when I say that it will last
You need not have a doubt
I'll be there when you need me to
That's what it's all about

It's All Good

It's all good
If you know what I mean
The highs, the lows
The in betweens
I have everything
When I'm with you
When I'm not, I don't know
What to do

I think about you
Every day
You're with me then
Somehow, some way
I hate for us
To be apart
But you are always
In my heart

And if you ask me
What will be
I'll say that if
It's up to me
I'd be with you
And when I could
I'd prove to you that
It's all good

I Remembered...

I saw you there waiting for me in your car, outside on a Winter's day. You looked up, our eyes met and you smiled and I remembered...

We spoke for a little while. I put my arm around your neck. I held your hand and our lips met. I looked deep into your eyes, where my world lives. You smiled and I remembered...

As we had our lunch, we talked. We held hands whenever the waiter left. I took my shoe off, so I could touch your foot under the table. We kissed. You met my gaze with one that was the same and you smiled and I remembered...

You went outside to have a smoke. I paid the check and said goodbye to smiles that said,"thanks for coming" and "hope to see you soon". We went to the car to say goodbye and we held each other close. I didn't want to let you go; but I did. As you drove away our eyes met and you smiled and I remembered...

Lost Love

Lost love
never was
only imagined

Strong pain
in my heart
what a fool!

Desperately trying
to understand
what for?

Wishing that
I didn't feel
so torn apart

No more tears
will ever fall
none left

Can't wait
to feel the pain
again tomorrow

If Only You

If only you
Would tell me why
Then I would never
Have to try

To figure out
Just what went wrong
To write another
Sad sad song

About a love
That broke my heart
That never finished
From a start

So glorious
I have to say
That even up
Until today

Has never seen
It's equal yet
I'm sure it never
Will I bet

And such a fire
Burned its flame
To you it only
Was a game

To me it was
My heart and soul
And when it finished
Took its toll

Upon my heart
Until this day
And it will never
Fade away

I thought that I
Was through with it
I don't think it
Will ever quit

And why it ended
I don't know
I'd hoped that you
Would tell me so

So I won't suffer
I won't cry
If only you
Would tell me why

Come to Me

Come to me, my love
And I will remind you
Why the sun rises each morning
And the moon at night
Why the clouds in the sky
Bring rain in the Summer
And snow in the Winter
There is but one reason to exist
Love is such a thing
Let me fill your face with kisses
And hold your body next to mine
A look becomes a hug
And a hug, a kiss
And a kiss brings that thing
That truly makes me understand
Why we exist at all
Come to me, my love

A Long Time Ago

A long time ago
But not so very far
I knew somehow that things
Would be just as they are

And my life would someday
Be the way it is now
Though I never knew why
Or just when, or just how

And the world wouldn't end
Though I thought that it would
'Cause you'll never come back
So I did what I could

To become what I am
Someone that I could say
Was worthwhile as the person
That I've become today

I have learned how to dance
And have wished on a star
That my love, I could send
To wherever you are

But you really don't want me
This I know to be true
And it just didn't matter
What I'd say or I'd do

That you just didn't love me
Now it all seems so clear
I was wasting my time
Till I cried my last tear

Now I'm stronger, you see
I won't act like a fool
What you did wasn't right
I don't think it was cool

That you made me believe
You could love me so strong
And that nothing else mattered
It could never be wrong

Then I cried and I cried
You had broken my heart
I just wanted to die
When I knew we would part

And that never again
Would a love be so true
That I never would feel
The way I did for you

It's the closest to fabulous
I'll ever be
But I guess you just didn't
Feel that way about me

So why do I remember
This old heartache tonight
And remember the things
That I thought weren't right

Because now I can say
That a long time ago
I am sure that I loved you
I just want you to know

To forgive someone's sins
Is a gift that's divine
And that I'll forgive yours
If you will forgive mine

That it's not all your fault
I know I'm to blame too
My unreasonable actions
Made you say we were through

And now we are both strangers
Haven't spoken for years
But I recall the passion
And remember the fears

Our love would be uncovered
And despised by our friends
They say flames that burn brightly
Are just dust when it ends

And so what it once was
Now is all in the past
They say all the best things
Are the ones that don't last

The Gift

If tomorrow you got on a plane
That flew you 'cross the sea
I'd still have all the memories
Of days of you and me
Of all the things that I would have
The feeling that runs deep
Is that I have one precious gift
That I can always keep

It's nothing that your eyes can see
And this, your hands can't hold
But I will have this special gift
To keep 'till I am old
It's not like it's a fantasy
It's real, I know it's true
You've given back a part of me
For years, I thought was through

The twinkle that was in my eye
The swagger in my walk
I see it in the mirror now
I hear it when I talk
I know it is an attitude
Towards my life, I guess
But ordinary just won't do
I have to have the best

And fabulous is what I want
I cannot settle now
And good enough is not enough
I want it all somehow
So if you ask,"what is this gift?"
Then I can only say
You've given back a part of me
I thought had gone away

If I Had a Christmas Wish

If I had a Christmas wish
Only one that would come true
I'd be closing both my eyes
And my thoughts would be of you

Doen't matter what you think
Doesn't matter what you say
This is my wish to enjoy
As I think of you today

I'd be nestled by a fire
On my chest your head would lay
As we finished our champagne
You would say, "oh what a day!"

As I held you oh so close
We'd be lying near our tree
As we heard the Christmas music
You'd be whispering to me

All the words to all the carols
Of those favorite Christmas songs
I would be oh so delighted
I'd just have to sing along

As we gazed into each other's eyes
There would have to be a trace
Of that joyous Christmas spirit
On your quiet, smiling face

And the only Christmas present
I would ever want from you
Is that when I say, "I love you"
You would say you love me too

Undying Love

How do I know if you love me?
Will there be a sign?
Or will I wake up one day and
just know it
I'm not sure
of anything
Confusion possesses me
It clings to me like the rain
on a hot Summer day
And all my clothes are wet
But at the same time I sweat
And I think
Could this be the real thing?
Or am I kidding myself
I face my own mortality
And wonder what was the purpose
Having been so sure
And so wrong
So many times before
Now I proceed on the premise
That I know nothing
That I have never been right
Only wrong
It consumes my thoughts
Yet I wonder
Does it really matter?
Or is this a fool's task
I know my mission
And here I am
Trying to discover
Undying Love

How Quickly You Forget

How quickly you forget
Those days not far behind
The mornings filled with glory
And afternoons so fine

But things not meant to be
Are only for a while
I think about it sometimes
It always makes me smile

And you compare to nothing
I've ever known before
If only I could find a way
To live it all once more

But Summer came and went
And then into the Fall
I really don't know why you left
I thought we had it all

And Christmas in the city
Seems like our last goodbye
I gaze upon my office wall
A view from in the sky

Of places we will never see
As I once dreamed we would
I can't imagine any more
I don't think that I should

But if I close my eyes
I still can see your face
The memory still calls me
Back to that special place

Where you and I once lived
A time without regret
Those days of love and passion
How quickly you forget

One Petal at a Time

It falls from the rose
One petal at a time
Like love from the heart
When I thought you'd be mine

But the days weren't kind
And the nights were so cold
And my love will remember
Till some day when I'm old

When the petals are gone
There remains, just the thorn
And the realization
That for which I was born

It's to live and to love
Someone with all my might
Till my heart, it stops beating
Till my eyes have no sight

But there's blood on the petals
Those that have not fell yet
For the one that I love
That I'll never forget

Night Song

It was never good, it was great
Fabulous, all the way
I cannot recall how life was
before you were part of mine
Sweet, loving, tender,
merciless, brutal, all at the
same time
I close my eyes, I can't sleep
I think of you every waking moment
There is nothing; only you
Who can stand to look at the Sun?
I hold you and the world stops
turning
It is truer than myself
No thoughts that can ever
become words
My destiny is but a second away
Who can hold the wind?
Stop sunrise, do not come
I pray these feelings do not
make me mad
My dark side has taken over
And yet all in my life is
goodness, sweetness, happiness
And as I drive myself
The nighttime surrounds me
To take me to the place
that I love so much
I can be myself, and live
And call you again
For tonight is tomorrow
And our love has survived
another day

No One Will Ever Know

No one will ever know
I'll take it to my grave
I never felt so low
Or knew how I'd behave
The secret I still keep
And promised not to tell
Cost me a lot of sleep
I put myself through hell

To try and win your heart
Was all that I could do
Until we had to part
You were my dream come true
And all that time, I tried
To be your closest friend
Believed you when you lied
Said it was not the end

I did not understand
Why you could not love me
You had the upper hand
I was too blind to see
You said no one could know
About our love affair
The places we did go
Were way beyond compare

I never was alive
Until I felt your touch
Somehow, I still survive
Without feeling too much
And when you had to go
Took back the love you gave
No one will ever know
I'll take it to my grave

Bon Voyage

I lost you many years ago
But you stayed in my heart, you know
And there was comfort still, I'd say
To know you weren't far away
I hear you're leaving here for good
But I have never understood
Just why we couldn't work it out
You didn't know what love's about

And now you never will, I guess
But there's one thing I must confess
That I will always love you so
I wish you didn't have to go
I can't forget the time we had
The way it ended made me mad
But fabulous, those days gone by
I'd like to give it one more try

And yet I'm sure it wouldn't work
Sometimes I feel like such a jerk
To fall in love the way I did
And carry on just like a kid
There was a gift you gave to me
I have my life back now, you see
There's nothing more for me to tell
Before it was a living hell

And it was you who set me free
You showed me all my life could be
And now I'm happy, more or less
I've gotten on with things, I guess
We'll never know what could have been
I'm happy that you were my friend
So Bon Voyage, be on your way
I hope we meet again some day

Why I Love July

I feel lost
Miles from home
I cannot recall your laugh
Or the smell of your body
I am not sure
Which way to go
I have forgotten everything
And yet I know
It wouldn't take much
for me to remember
The touch of your hand
A look into your eyes
Five minutes later
It would all come back
Like a rush of cool air
Or a Summer's rain
In July
The sweetest of months

My Dreams Are Still of You

So would it have been wonderful?
It would have been the best
If only I was not afraid
To put it to the test

I thought you didn't want me
I thought you didn't care
It seems to me that sometimes
The world is so unfair

But I remember all the times
I still remember when
Those days seem oh so long ago
I still like to pretend

That you and I are still as one
With hearts that beat in time
We shared the hopes, we shared the dreams
That one day you'd be mine

And late at night, when I'm asleep
Somehow I think it's true
That as I lie there, sound asleep
My dreams are still of you

The Muse

The way the Sun
Shined on your hair
Inspired me
To even dare
Put all my feelings
In a song
Although I knew
That it was wrong

When Love had left
Me all alone
The Blues that made
Me weep and moan
Was inspiration
That helped me
To write the words
That set me free

So many hours
I did try
To finally
Tell you goodbye
It really did
Become my goal
To soothe the pain
Within my soul

I cannot write
A song today
That was as good
As yesterday
My poetry
So filled with pain
Will never be
The same again

And Love is like
An empy shell
Forgetting you
Put me through Hell
I know, I'll never
Be the same
I only have
Myself to blame

But all the years
I suffered through
Made me do what
I had to do
And so, I wrote
My sad refrain
It really made me
Use my brain

The work I did
Turned out to be
The best thing that
There was for me
I feel the magic
Of those years
In words, I wrote
To dry my tears

I guess I owe
So much to you
You sure taught me
A thing or two
You were my Muse
For oh so long
I hardly ever
Wrote a song

That I was not
Inspired to
By all the things
That I went through
And as a poet
I arrived
Through all the heartache
I survived

The worse I felt
The more I tried
To understand
Why you had lied
I thought you'd always
Be my friend
Believed our love
Would never end

I never knew
You'd be so cruel
It made me feel
Like such a fool
Still, all the things
I wrote about
They all were true
I have no doubt

I was in love
All by myself
You put my love
Out on a shelf
And never thought
About it twice
The way you were
Was cold as ice

The best work, I
Will ever do
Has been because
What I went through
We all have felt
The pain of Love
And everything
I've written of

I probably
Owe to my Muse
I can't escape it
What's the use
Without a cause
There is no verse
And are no words
This is my curse

Now that you're gone
This time for good
I'm starting to
Feel like I should
And happiness
Is okay too
But leaves me with
Not much to do

The pain I felt
Was like a friend
I thought I'd have
Until the end
Although I don't
Miss the abuse
I'm lost for words
Without my Muse

A Different Kind of Love

It's a different kind
Of love, you see
The kind that we have
You and me
I'm not sure what
It's all about
But I know I
Will never doubt
The way you feel
It's oh so strong
I'm sure that I
Cannot be wrong
I feel it when
I am asleep
It's something that
I'll always keep
Inside my heart
Until the end
You'll always be
That special friend
And as a lover
You're the best
I know I can
Forget the rest
I only hope
That one fine day
The love we have
Will find a way
To bring our hearts
So close that we
Can feel them beating
Don't you see
This gift we have
Comes from above
A truly different

Kind of love
No one has ever
Felt the way
I feel about you
I must say
That Fame and Fortune
Are okay
But can't compare
Not with the way
I feel with each breath
That I take
And wonder how
That I can make
You happy every
Single day
I know I'd like
To find a way
The riches I
Can live without
But you know I
Will never doubt
That I need you
To be with me
'Cause only you
Can set me free
I cannot hide
The way I feel
The love I have
Is just too real
This is the stuff
Dreams are made of
A truly different
Kind of love

I Thought About You

I thought about you
On a cold Winter's night
And wondered if I
Could have made it all right

I thought about you
Every word, every song
I had written about
How you treated me wrong

I thought about you
Did I still feel the same?
How it all went to hell
And that I was to blame

I thought about you
As I lay in my bed
Wondering what had I done
Was it something I said?

I thought about you
And it made me feel fine
Until I realized
That you never were mine

Fall From the Sky

Fall from the sky, stars
Let the world end
It has no meaning
Without you in it
You will be gone soon
I feel it in my heart
Never to be seen again
Only thought about
And to be missed
By one lonely heart
Who never got over you
And never will

I will try till my last breath
To forget the love I had
I was in love alone
A terrible place to be
So, if the world ends
I will not care
My misery will be done
And the pain will exist no more

To feel the way I do
Makes everything seem pointless
And nothing is important
So why try at all
I'm so very tired
But I cannot sleep
Thoughts of you fill my head
Until it almost explodes

The only way to stop it
Is for everything to cease
And Eternity to begin
Starting from emptiness
It will have no ending
Until nothing else exists
Till the Sun shines no more
The Earth stops turning
Time and Space collide
And I am no more

Indifferent Homicide

When a person tries to answer love
With an attitude of who may care
It's the worst thing that I can think of
Nothing that for which you can prepare

Everything that I remember now
That you did to cause my heart to die
I am sure you knew some way, somehow
How your love for me was all a lie

If you didn't care at all for me
How did I believe you loved me so
It was all I hoped that it would be
Till the time I knew that you would go

So you went and you left me behind
Guess I should have seen you were untrue
Somehow I thought I had lost my mind
When I realized that we were through

There's a lesson to be learned from this
It took me so long to find it out
That you can't be sure from just one kiss
You will ever know what Love's about

The Color Blue

The colors in my mind
Blend together into one color; blue
For blue is the color of my baby
Through it I see all things
And it gives its richness to everything
in my life
I could sleep for a hundred years
But when I awaken, I would still
feel the same
It makes me ache in my stomach
Yet my vision is smooth and refreshed
Another color is completely different
And as I feel it today, I know it is totally
unlike anything I have ever felt in my life
It runs through my blood
And permeates the air that fills my lungs
Ah blue, blue, I breathe you in, but I
do not exhale
Because I hope to keep this feeling
Forever

Love's Surrender

Tonight a last attempt was made
Remembering the days of you
And all the things I thought were true
Somehow my mind does now evade
The way I looked deep in your eyes
At promises that all were lies

I try, but I cannot recall
Those feelings that were oh so strong
Imagining them felt so wrong
It seems it wasn't real at all
Now I don't see you any more
Things are not like they were before

A wish was made upon a star
Somehow that I'd be in your arms
To know the sweetness of your charms
But it just never got that far
I guess I could give you a call
But then I'm sure I'd want it all

Suppose I just try to forget
The way we made each other feel
Then you and I will make a deal
Pretend it isn't over yet
And dream of things we're thinking of
Because we've given up on love

Part III

The Gypsy

Sorrowful Living

Living in sorrow
Always in pain
Can't keep from crying
Again and again
Try to remember
When life was good
Got what I needed
All that I could

Never was happy
With what I had
My expectations
Just made me mad
I'm oh so tired
Still I can't sleep
Thinking of promises
I couldn't keep

Over and over
Never was right
Only was happy
When I would fight
I was unfaithful
Never believed
All the illusions
I had conceived

All the pollution
Soon took it's toll
Until my life went
Out of control
Something in my heart
Told me to quit
Nothing that I tried
Helped me a bit

I landed softly
Into my bed
Luckily, I landed
Right on my head
You'd think that I may
Have gained some sense
Total stupidity
That's my defense

Filled lots of pages
Writing about
All of the things
I knew nothing about
Living in sorrow
I'm not done yet
I'll be done crying
Someday, I'll bet

Dark Thoughts (A Vampire's Prayer)

Dark are the thoughts in my head
I hear evil whispered in my ear
It says to drink of the blood again
Even though it almost killed you
It gives you life
And it controls your soul
You cannot escape it
It is every thought you have
To begin again as before
You cannot say no to it
It is your reason for existing
Even now, you smell it
The aroma intoxicates your mind
It is without conscience
Like the animal who kills
Because it is what it needs to do
And I am of such a mind
I long to caress a neck
That will give me my life's blood
To exist in darkness
But to have life again
I will surely die without it
And my soul is condemned
To never see the daylight
I will hear and see and breathe
Within a new life
That calls my soul towards it
I am no longer myself
I am once again with you
To be yours only
Together we will burn
In the fire of Eternity

The Poet's Words

Speak
Only words
Can reveal
What's inside
What is real

Share
Other eyes
Cannot see
Things I feel
Within me

Feel
Embrace pain
Sometimes cry
You'll find love
If you try

Create
It is yours
Be unique
Give others
What they seek

Live
Life goes on
When you're dead
They'll recall
What you said

In the Shadows

It is late as I stagger
Into the drunken crowd
The noise envelopes me
I am greeted as a friend
Recognition commences
Honored and respected
A toast to the reverie here
The end of a long night

Suddenly I am summoned
Further intoxication calls me
It beckons me to partake
I am helpless to resist
Firewater fills my veins
My new friend, filled with delight
Not by the bottle in his hand
He pays no attention to the music

It is a celebration of life
We have become the party
Then suddenly I see her
At first, he keeps her hidden
But she cannot be missed
Her beauty peeks through
Then she shines like the Sun
When the rain clouds roll away

There she sits in the corner
Hardly able to be seen
Dark in the shadows
But, radiant as she is
It is impossible not to see her
How she shows her beauty
Overwhelms all my senses
And has captured my imagination

I Have Grown to Love You

I have grown to love you, baby
With all of my heart and soul
I can see us both together
In the years that we are old

And my time is almost finished
I will want you by my side
And our love, it will continue
Even after we have died

For you fill my heart completely
I have learned to love so well
And I feel it so completely
Things that others only tell

You're the reason for my laughter
And the sparkle in my eye
I'm complete when I am with you
And our love is not a lie

For I could not live without you
Don't know how I could go on
But I'm really not quite sure
What our love is based upon

You're the opposite of what
I expect a girl to be
And I don't think you're quite sure
What it is, you see in me

Still, my heart is filled with joy
At the mention of your name
I knew since the day I met you
That I'll never be the same

When I wake up in the morning
And I have you by my side
I know I can face the world
Now I can say, that I've tried

Everything I've ever wanted
I know that, my life, I'd bet
On the love that's grown so precious
Since the day that we first met

For What of This Curse?

For what of this curse
That seems to be
A force of the Past
That has sent me
Back to my youth
Into my dreams
I feel it now
Or so it seems

It came to me
Last night, you see
From ancient times
To a city
That's far from here
And long ago
It's surfaced now
For me to know

I did somebody
Wrong it said
I must atone
Or I'll be dead
Forgiveness, then
I ask of you
So finally
It will be through

And yet forgiveness
Granted me
Would not dispel
This thing to me
I try to run
It follows fast
As if this step
Will be my last

And when this dream
Is over, then
I stay awake
Till God knows when
Afraid to sleep
The light stays on
As if the demons
All had won

Tonight it's late
But now I dread
That when I finally
Am in bed
The nightmare will
Come back to me
I wish that I
Would just be free

Never again
To feel the fear
And that my slumber
Would be clear
And it is lifted
From my heart
I don't know where
To even start

To tell you of
The misery
And of that which
Has come to me
One night of fear
It haunts my soul
I'm not so sure
I can control

The horrid thoughts
I fear tonight
And I can never
Make it right
Unless, of course
I pray to God
And ask Him if
He finally could

Protect me if
It's not too late
I know this cannot
Be my fate
To finally die
With Hope no more
To enter through
The Final Door

And never know
Just what I did
When I was only
Just a kid
To con jour spirits
From below
That chase me now
Here to and fro

Till finally
I cannot run
I stay awake
Until the Sun
Comes back again
And a new day
Will take me somewhere
Far away

From all this anguish
That I feel
I know it's nothing
That is real
And still I felt
With all my might
That I would perish
Late last night

The Party

There was Music
There was Singing
There was Beer
There was Wine
There was Cake
There was Ice Cream
There was Laughter
There was Conversation
There was Fun
There were Flowers
There were People
There were Hugs
There were Kisses
There were Hellos
There were Goodbyes
There was Everything
Except You

Cruisin'

Cruisin', you and me
It's become routine
Tell me what you think
I don't know what you mean

When you say you hate me
Do you love me too?
I'm not sure I know
What I feel for you

Things are always changing
Somehow, you and me
Now are rearranging
What's supposed to be

Will you always love me?
I'm not sure you will
You are always moving
And you won't stand still

But I've realized
Life can hold for you
Many more surprises
Than you want it to

Wake up in the morning
Go to bed at night
Spent no time together
Didn't even fight

It was nothing special
Anyone could see
Things are going badly
We're not meant to be

Kind of makes me wonder
What I'm doing here
You won't miss me baby
I won't shed a tear

I'm not feelin' nothin'
Not enough to care
You're not goin' nowhere
You just wouldn't dare

You and I are cruisin'
Don't believe we're done
When you think it's finished
It has just begun

The Gypsy

It makes me wonder
Makes me sad
Remembering things
That we once had
When I recall
The days gone by
It always makes me
Want to cry

The Gypsy comes
The Gypsy goes
And no one ever
Really knows
Just why they act
The way they do
They're really not
Like me and you

One day they're here
The next, they're gone
It's simply time
That they move on
And love is something
That they feel
But you can't say
It's ever real

There's no possession
That they need
There's nothing that
They need indeed
And I once loved one
This is true
But there was nothing
I could do

But let her go
One day I did
She won't be back
No, God forbid
My life has changed
So much since then
I really don't
Remember when

I couldn't wait
To see her face
The way I felt
Was a disgrace
And now I see
The Gypsy life
Was never ro
Become a wife

It's not the way
The Gypsies live
I understand
I must forgive
My heart for being
Such a fool
And now I know
It wasn't cool

To cage a bird
That needs to fly
And I just had
To blink my eye
She's gone, you know
I didn't see
That Life's a game
For the Gypsy

The Truth About the Truth

You think it's hot
Or maybe cold
It isn't young
But, oh so old

And every day
You hope it's found
Till finally
It comes around

The Truth, it has
No temperature
That's by design
You can be sure

Although you think
You know it well
Sometimes it's very
Hard to tell

Some people lie
To make things right
Sometimes, so they
Don't have to fight

But in the end
It shall prevail
Unto the very
Last detail

It's inconvenient
Sometimes to
Admit to something
That is true

A lie's a lie
Till we admit
It's said for our
Own benefit

The lesson here
For all to see
Is that the truth
Will set you free

Rendezvous

Came to me last night
Everything felt right
Filled my heart with song
Can't believe it's wrong
I felt your desire
Passion's burning fire
Stayed with me till morning
I ignored the warning

Since you've been away
I've cried every day
Love will never die
Only pass you by
Said you have to go
Though I loved you so
You came back to see
What you missed in me

And I played your game
Yes, I feel the same
Making love to you
Like you want me to
Now I'm feeling sad
For the thing we had
Isn't really gone
Let's just say it's done

But I feel the pain
Now you're gone again
You are like no other
My forever lover
One more time, it seems
You've fulfilled my dreams
Except, that now I'm blue
From our rendezvous

Alone

Driving down the road today
Thinking that I'm happy now
I don't miss you every day
Feel I'm better off somehow

Living by myself right now
Don't need any company
I'll embrace the solitude
Only have to think of me

Sleeping in my bed at night
Hoping that someday I will
Feel somebody next to me
Thinking that I love you still

It's my choice to be this way
Told you that you had to go
Didn't think I needed you
Even though I loved you so

Woke up with the Sun today
Staring at the telephone
Nobody will bother me
Now I'm happy, I'm alone

Elegance

She's poised and graceful
Has all the right angles
Moves like a breeze
On a hot Summer's day
The light in her eyes
Shines through from her mind
Her lips remain closed
But poised to strike quickly

There are many nevers
Just as there are always
Grace comes easily
Restraint always prevails
Everything is well thought out
Nothing is left to chance
She remains attainable
Although somewhat distant

Her intentions are made known
Without being overstated
Her confidence shines
Never needing assistance
She can read people
By their actions, not words
Isn't wrong very often
But not afraid to admit it

You like her immediately
Followed shortly by love
Women want to be her
Men are instantly mesmerized
Learns from her mistakes
Doesn't have to be told twice
Realizes her shortcomings
Makes the best of what she has

Doesn't judge too quickly
Is able to change her mind
Always a good listener
Respects other's opinions
Isn't afraid of criticism
Continuously tries to improve
Always makes the best of things
By constantly preparing for the worst

In Despair

There is nothing worse
Than the pain of rejection
Slow, torturous
It sends me into despair
I don't care if the world ends
Or what happens to me
I am totally numb
And I walk in sleep
I don't want to go on
And continue like this
Death seems merciful
Compared to the pain I feel
Even the sound of your voice
Does nothing to calm me
I do not even desire
The happiness I once felt
I only wish one thing
To be alone in my despair
And to take comfort
In the fact that I am alone
Nobody can hurt me now

Love and Hate

The world is love
But full of hate
I take a breath
And say, why wait
For both will come
To you the same
As if you knew
It was a game

That you knew well
Sometimes you did
When you were acting
Like a kid
I say to you
That both extremes
Go way too far
Or so it seems

Like pride and hurt
Go hand in hand
Sometimes it's more
Than you can stand
Of all the things
I ever knew
It was the pain
Inside that grew

And those extremes
I realized
Sometimes they had me
Hypnotized
I didn't see
I couldn't hear
Then all at once
It was so clear

A moment lost
Which I had found
Quite suddenly
Turned things around
I found out that
What I was sold
Was not the truth
That I was told

When I awoke
As one who dreams
Nothing was real
Or so it seems
I found out when
It all was done
That Love and Hate
Are really one

Living the Dream

My life, it is not as it would seem
Contentment seems so far
One day I'll break away from here
And drive off in my car

I'm headed down to New Orleans
My music cannot wait
I'll play all night and sleep all day
Before it is too late

I've thought about it for so long
It's now a part of me
The land of Cajon melodies
Is what I long to see

I think about the Mardigras
I hear it takes the cake
I've dreamed about it all my life
Even when I'm awake

But something that is in my soul
When I play with a band
It takes me to a place so high
I never want to land

And here's a clue to all of you
Who never played a note
You only have to feel the groove
To get what I just wrote

The Legend of Don José

If only you had known him
You'd know this story's true
The only part he left us
Lives on in me and you
A brother to his friends
The women, he made smile
There wasn't anyone I knew
That he could not beguile

The legend still survives
Though it's been many years
When hundreds of us said goodbye
With laughter and with tears
The church was full, you had to stand
So many people came
But there was nothing but the ice
That we could ever blame

Then when it all was over
We got together to
All drink a final toast and say;
"José, this one's for you"
I never have met anyone
Whose personality
Made everyone admire him
That's what he did to me

I saw him almost every day
All spotless and shipshape
The way the Don carried himself
That no one could escape
His uniform was always pressed
The hat, a perfect fit
His hair, it had the perfect cut
Now that I think of it

And when you saw that smile
A perfect row of pearl
He knew just how to steal the heart
Of every single girl
To tell you that I loved him
Is simply not enough
I never saw such tenderness
From somebody so tough

He got me out of trouble
More than a time or two
You only had to let him know
And he'd be there for you
His home in Puerto Rico
We promised we would go
He said he had a trip in mind
That just we two would know

Those Caribbean sunsets
He liked to talk about
And that he loved that Island
I never had a doubt
We planned our big vacation
Adventure, it would seem
But we would never get there
It only was a dream

It was so unexpected
When he died in the cold
Alone, the Black Ice took him
Before he could grow old
I'm always melancholy
When I think of my friend
And on that Sunny Island
He wound up in the end

Fright Night

Things that go bump in the night
Sometimes, they give me a fright
Tried to be brave when I dared
I admit, sometimes I'm scared

Some things I just can't explain
I'm afraid they'll cause me pain
I'll hear a noise or a sound
Wonder if ghosts are around

Then I'm afraid of the dark
Or if I hear a dog bark
Often it doesn't make sense
Feelings that seem so intense

Watching those shows on T.V.
Sure scares the Hell out of me
When I am home all alone
I'm horrified to the bone

Then, when I'm out in the sticks
Sometimes my mind will play tricks
I know that none of it's real
It doesn't help how I feel

I'm creeped out, I must confide
If I hear noises outside
I know it's all in my head
Still, I'm scared to go to bed

Outside

I lost my job
Couldn't pay the rent
Had to move out
Only had money for food
Slept in my car
Couldn't buy gas
Had to sell that too

My wife left me
Took the kids
It's only me now
Ran out of everything
Not looking so good
People look away from me
Lost my self respect

Learned about life
Even on the street
Everyone has an agenda
Don't trust anyone
Kindness is weakness
Learned to beg for change
Drank to kill the pain

Scared of everybody
Don't trust the police
Found the soup kitchen
Politics, even there
Everybody lies
Slept in a dumpster
Got robbed in a shelter

Learned to travel light
Don't talk to anyone
Alone every night
Stay in the shadows
Woke up one morning
And I found myself
Living outside

The King of West Babylon

Where have you gone
Oh Mighty King
Whose life upon
I do now sing
Beloved days
Of misspent youth
I give you praise
And tell your truth
You left one day
Ne'er to return
Are gone to stay
So I would learn
When someone said
That you were dead

Because we're done
With days gone past
The friends we've won
Sometimes don't last
But still you stay
Inside my heart
You've gone away
For'er apart
I wrote to you
Without reply
Then I found out
The reason why
You never tried
Because you died

The days and nights
At Oak Beach Inn
Filled with delights
Sometimes with sin
You stood around
Watched drunkards dance
Always were found
In regal stance
As if the show
Were just for you
You'd always know
Just what to do
You were so cool
Nobody's fool

We'd never leave
Till it was four
They had to throw
Us out the door
Then we'd drive home
On the Causeway
Where ocean foam
Shines on the bay
Somehow alive
We did prevail
And would survive
To tell the tale
That I now sing
Of thee, my King

This Dream Called Life

Sometimes, I don't think that I am awake
Reality's what seems to be at stake
It's in this world, I feel like I reside
And in this slumber, I must always stay
The strangeness and confusion, I abide
As I meander through another day
Oh, say that one day I'll arise
And leave behind what I despise

There are no words to tell you how I feel
When things occur that somehow don't seem real
The places in my mind I travel to
Reflect the problems that I must control
The odd things that I somehow need to do
That help defense my unprotected soul
When things are not like they would seem
I'm in a never ending dream

When in the future, I attempt to see
I travel there to where I want to be
Then back in time, I seem myself to find
In days of old with people who I love
I realize, I've left them all behind
But still they are the ones I'm thinking of
And all that's happened in the past
Becomes so clear to me, at last

So, when my words connect just like a song
And I feel like I'd hoped to for so long
Emotions I express that are so deep
I've hidden from the world until just now
Exposing secrets I have tried to keep
That take on their own life someway, somehow
It all compels me to partake
Of dreams that come when I'm awake

The Secret of the Blind Man

He's well dressed and dashing
Always wears his shades
Hears you coming early
Sometimes, he evades

You wonder how it feels
To live without your eyes
With what you think you know
It's all this, he defies

He's many different people
Each one unlike the rest
But every one superb
That's what he likes the best

When everyone who sees
Thinks they have more than he
But have not realized that
He's all he wants to be

And if you knew his secret
You'd marvel even more
How in his world of darkness
Somehow he's keeping score

One thing we can be sure of
Is that his heart's delight
Comes when he is admired
By people who have sight

The Circle

No matter where it all begins
The circle goes back to the start
With every motion, every turn
Each one of us must play their part
With eyes that see all that's around
But cannot see too far behind
Reality confronts us all
But cannot infiltrate our mind

It starts the day that we are born
The clock is ticking till we die
Our purpose on this Earth's not clear
We never know the reason why
And so we live from day to day
To find direction in our life
There's so much we're uncertain of
We live our days in pain and strife

Then one day when our journey ends
Just when we think there's nothing more
It's then, the circle is complete
Or will we find another door
That opens to another world
Where each of us can find relief
The circle goes back to the start
But only if you have belief

Part IV

Awaken, My Heart

This Feeling

Love
Have I really been
Transported by you
Into another world
Where everything is
Wonderful and new
I wake up every day
Embrace the morning
Another chance to feel
The happiness you bring
And every night
I fall asleep
In the arms of ecstasy
Until my slumber
Mingles with my dreams
And I no longer can tell
Which one is reality
This feeling I have
Is beyond comprehension
There is no understanding
Only emotion
That dwells inside
To the very depths
Of my soul

Ruthie

Where have you been all my life
I would have made you my wife
It comes as such a surprise
To see my world in your eyes
Under the full moon that night
I felt like things were just right

We took a walk on the beach
Your love was just out of reach
You came to me in my dreams
I fell for you, so it seems
Can't help the way that I feel
Wonder if this is for real

Once in a while you can see
Things as they are meant to be
I felt that way from the start
You have the key to my heart
I never met you before
I knew that I wanted more

You came and brightened my day
Must have been your sexy way
The sky by the moon was so clean
Nothing like I'd ever seen
Caught in the warmth of your smile
I think that I'll stay a while

Let Me Try

Oh, let me try
To write for you
The perfect lines
To tell you so

Oh, let me try
To sing for you
The perfect song
So you will know

Oh, let me try
To play for you
The perfect notes
So you can hear

Oh, let me try
To show to you
The perfect thoughts
To make things clear

Oh, let me try
To tell to you
The perfect story
One that is true

Oh, let me try
To speak to you
The perfect words
That I love you

Personal Poetry

I will not say that
I write poetry
With the idea that
It's just written for me
I'm not sure what I write
Is for others to see
Or I've written the words
Only for them to be

But then, I must confess
This is somehow a lie
Because why even write
If it isn't to try
To have others observe
As the world passes by
And express how they feel
Even if they must cry

We have all felt emotions
That we know others do
And we just don't see them
From our own point of view
We need some validation
So we know that it's true
It has always been so
This is nothing that's new

So we try very hard
To say something that's right
About things we imagine
That are out of our sight
When we feel overwhelmed
Turn the darkness to light
So that we can tell others
Not to give up the fight

We can just let them know
That we really do care
There will always be hard times
And that life isn't fair
When it seems like it all
Is more than we can bear
There is something that helps
Overcome our despair

It's our personal poetry
There like a song
When you look in your heart
It won't take very long
Just believe in yourself
And you'll never be wrong
Let the words you create
Take you where you belong

Goodbye Misery

Oh, Misery
I once belonged to you
You had me in your spell
Every day and every night
You possessed my soul
I never did anything
Without thinking of you
First and foremost
You were on my mind
I ate and slept and drank
Under your complete control
Then something happened
Like running out of gas
It suddenly stopped
As if by magic
Time had finally won
It heals all wounds
Sooner or later
It conquers everything

Daddy's Songs

All night long, we'll sleep, he'll play
He sings the night into the day
We know he knows the words by heart
On his guitar, he'll play the part
Of Rock Star, playing songs of love
And all the things that he sings of
His broken heart, his joy, his pain
He says he'll never love again

But you can tell what's in his soul
It's in his music, he feels whole
His saddest songs can make you cry
He says he'll give it one more try
And love again, you know he will
He just cannot resist the thrill
He'll say he's lonesome every night
And won't give up without a fight
Sometimes he sings like he will die
He watches as the world goes by

It's all these things he feels inside
That other people try to hide
He puts out there, that we may see
All of the things we want to be
These feelings we have every day
And pain that never goes away
So sleep tight children, dream along
While Daddy sings another song

My Perfect Night

My perfect night
It was a sight
A dream I dreamed
Came true, it seemed
And so I fell
Into your spell
My heart's delight
At your first sight

I must insist
I knew I'd missed
Most of my life
Without a wife
Who'd be so good
I hoped she would
Come rescue me
And set me free

The moon above
Shone bright as love
So we could see
How it might be
Like we are now
Married, somehow
No one would bet
When we first met

We'll be together
Now and forever
You stole my heart
I did my part
To make you mine
You were so fine
We took a walk
There was some talk

What had I missed
We had not kissed
But I knew then
That only when
I could have you
To see me through
I'd finally feel
That Love was real

I loved you so
From the word go
It's really true
You know it too
That from that night
It's been all right
And by the sea
You too, loved me

Beyond Belief

How high, how high
Your cliffs go on forever
Without limit, it seems
The place of the world's end
I see a bird fly sweetly
It catches my attention
Soaring serenely overhead
At the ceiling of The Canyon
Beyond where, my imagination
Has ever dared to journey
Only to be believed
As one witnesses a miracle

I stand as a tiny insect
Where distance cannot be measured
The drum of the Native people
Calls everyone to come hear
At dusk, he comes to visit
That great creature from the forest
Magnificent in his size
An elegant figure against the night
I am unable to sleep
As I wander the great hall, alone

At dawn, they will arrive here
To greet the new day with humility
The inhabitants of the entire world
Come here and feel your spirit
The wonder that has awakened
Becomes their very being
Their parade, a constant stream
Barely diminished by the rain
Expanding with the sunshine
A chance to capture the glory

As if taking her picture
Would somehow contain her essence
But failing to en capture
The wonderment of her presence

The glory of the sunrise
As it meets the new day
Shines its heavenly light
On the temple God has created
It fills your entire soul
As if you had partaken of
The wine that came from water
That Jesus himself changed
And all the pilgrims gather
To worship at the altar
Proclaiming their amazement
That such a place exists

Then, when the day is finished
The splendor of the sunset
Descending into shadows
And soon into the darkness
Where stars seem somewhat closer
Their purpose more compelling
My eyes become two windows
That look into my soul

I Try

I try to hide the pain
And do the best I can
It hurts down deep inside
Now here it comes again

I try to stop myself
From feeling like I do
I just don't think I will
Be able to get through

I try to keep from crying
The tears I have inside
No one can ever know
That my poor heart has died

I try to have a smile
That I keep on my face
But everything is gone
Some things you can't replace

I try to live my life
The way I have been told
Nobody ever said
The world would be so cold

Wedding Song
(for: Katie O.)

Fly to me
All those who love me
When I become one
With the man of my dreams
Who's so precious to me
I've waited for this
My whole life
It's like a Fairy Tale
My perfect day
I'm a woman now
All grown up
And ready to begin
My journey through life
Take food and drink
And celebrate with me
Let your feet move
While the music plays
Our first dance
As husband and wife
Everyone will watch
The magic we make
As we love each other
Like nobody else
Ever did or can
So special to me
That you all wish
To be here too
As we join together
In perfect union

The Jewel

I see your smile
The way the light hits your eyes
It glistens on your blond hair
You have a certain glow
It radiates throughout the night
And when I see your smile
The possibilities thrill me

I see the flowers here
Their long stems bend and curve
And at the very top
Their yellow petals are magnificent
They remind me of you
Beauty and grace together

You are in the Springtime of your life
Summer has already begun
But I am in Autumn
And I feel the cold is coming
Every night since I've met you
My dreams take me back to the past

I would have loved you then
But not as much as now
For you are a jewel
And the years enhance my appreciation
Of a mother and her small children
How someday they will be grown

And as much as I want you
I'm afraid that I'm out of time
For in twenty years you will be
More beautiful than ever
And I will be an old man
I couldn't bear to lose you

I haven't known you very long
But you have touched my heart
The sound of your voice talking
And your eyes speak to me
I forget who I really am
And why it could never be

I have so much to offer
But it's not meant to be
For you are a beautiful flower
A rose still on the vine
It would just be wrong
Not to leave it alone

Inner Demon

I'd hoped he may depart
But he saw me tonight
He lives within my heart
Sometimes stays out of sight

Disguised from me by day
I think I'm safe in love
At night he makes me pay
The worst he can think of

He's caused a lot of tears
I'm sure he isn't through
I've known him many years
He's quite the trickster, too

And when I hope he's gone
Just when my life is sweet
I can depend upon
My ultimate defeat

When I believed I'd found
The girl who was for me
My Demon came around
And had to disagree

When I think they're the one
Who'll love me like they should
One day it will be done
And they'll be gone for good

Why do I have this curse
To never be content
It can't be any worse
Where has all my love went

Cry

Cry
Find the tears
Feel the emotion
Don't question why
It's inside
Never wavering
Without conscience
It continues
Never ending
A far cry from
Being apathetic
It only knows
Yes and no
Do and don't
No one can control it
No one wants to
It is part of you
Always will be
A stream of emotion
Divided by days
And years from now
It's hardly recognizable
But it's still there
Think about it
Feel it again
Cry

While She Lays Sleeping

While she lays sleeping all alone
I try to bring my thoughts to light
And in the bedroom down the hall
In solitude, the words I write
That always seem to cleanse my soul
At night when I can't go to sleep
I take a journey through my head
Return from where my thoughts run deep
Sometimes I come back with the words
That satisfy my troubled mind
But other times it feels like I
Have left those answers far behind

Somewhere she's living in a dream
But I must wait until I feel
I've cleared my mind of all it's doubts
And helped my fragile heart to heal
There are no words to tell you why
It's just something I have to do
And now it's such a part of me
I don't know how I could get through
Those sleepless nights that come and go
When my words put my mind at rest
I don't think it will ever end
I'm on a never ending quest

Vision of Summer

When I awaken tomorrow
The day will be mine
Then I will make my pilgrimage
To the field of dreams
A cup of coffee to warm me
And out the door I go

I am just about an hour away
To be joined by forty thousand
Known to me as "the faithful"
As we gather together
To begin another year
A festival for the foolish
Who remain loyal to our calling

As we survey the stadium
The last remnants of the Winter
Blow over the new blades of grass
Decorated with our team's logo
I've dreamed of hot dogs
Eaten while drinking in
This year's crop of talent

And the roar of the crowd
Screaming in anticipation
Of the long season ahead
When we no longer require
Protection from the Winter
And our stadium attire
Becomes shorts and t-shirts

Free to soak up some rays
But careful to apply the sunscreen
Our shades will glisten
As we wipe the sweat from our brows
When the crack of the baseball bat
Is the sweetest sound we can hear

My Forever Love

I know you're out there somewhere
I've waited for so long
It's just like in my fantasies
And like a favorite song

Too few the moments in our lives
When everything is right
They seem to slip away so fast
Like day becomes the night

I hope that you will show up soon
I'm lonely as can be
Can't wait to hold you in my arms
Someday you'll be with me

Then I'll be happy, you will see
A man who is content
And I will thank the stars above
I'll say you're heaven sent

It's then, my dreams will all come true
These things I'm thinking of
For you'll be with me in my heart
My one, forever love

The Breakdown

I cry sometimes
Without much sense
And often it
Is so intense
The sadness that
I feel inside
Is something that
I try to hide

But it comes out
With no real cause
Controls me till
I must take pause
To stop myself
Or go insane
From how I feel
Inside my brain

Woke up today
Downstairs I crept
Then I got sad
And so I wept
I do not seem
To understand
How I keep things
So well in hand

In one moment
I feel that I
Am overwhelmed
And so I cry
I can't say how
I make it stop
Just after one
Or two tears drop

I get caught up
In all the pain
Until my strength
I can regain
Something tells me
To just sit down
Or I'll have a
Complete breakdown

Make Me Understand

Words cannot explain so well
When there's something that you must tell
Beyond the limits that we face
Confining all the human race
I think so hard before I write
So I can get the feeling right

There's so much more that I don't see
About the way things have to be
It's not supposed to be that way
A price so dear, that we must pay
But knowledge comes to those who wait
The Truth's what we anticipate

I learn the hard way every time
More difficult for words to rhyme
And yet some glimmer still shines through
Of what I am supposed to do
I hope that Fate will lend a hand
So I will finally understand

Awaken, My Heart

Awaken, my heart
And live once more
Become as you
Once were before
So long ago
You were so true
In every thing
You'd say and do

With each day now
You're more alive
I don't know how
I did survive
Without your help
I'd be a mess
I'd wither up
And die, I guess

For many years
You've been asleep
Afraid of any
Love so deep
But now it's time
To try and be
All that you can
You've got to see

You will become
My guiding light
And you'll be here
Both day and night
To show me which
Way I should go
And all the things
That I should know

I feel you now
You're beating strong
And you've come back
Where you belong
You realize
It's love I need
To demonstrate
With word and deed

I didn't think
That you'd be back
To show me what
It is I lack
The feeling that
There's something good
I'd sing about it
If I could

I only know
That love is real
The way I know
Is how I feel
And every day
I feel it stronger
I won't be lonely
Any longer

And all those years
That you forgot
You were so cold
But now you're hot
You're not asleep
For heaven's sake
It's only now
You are awake

So now you know
It's not a dream
Your time has come
So it would seem
This gift to you
Comes from above
Awaken, my heart
You are in love

O Passionate Love

O Passionate Love
Where hast thou gone?
When I would wake
With the power in my soul
To spend my days
Waiting to meet thee
And feel thee with me
In the pit of my stomach
An ache that no longer survives

But, as a fire dies down
Its ambers retain the heat
Until what remains is only
Slightly warm and gray
I find thee and lose thee
Whether time or circumstance
Distracts me from thee
I wander too far away
And it simply vanishes
I pray that it returns

But Reality overwhelms me
I have felt thee before
My understanding is limited
Wilt thou ever return?
My fear grows stronger that thou won't
Then I recognize my old companion looming
He is Loneliness; a sad relation
I do not acknowledge him
Hoping that he will not stay long
Do I ask for too much?
Should I settle for Contentment?
There is much happiness with her

Maybe I am like the Widower
Who only remembers the good times
Although I understand her departure
I still believe that she is with me
Love that outlives Death itself
The notion intrigues me
I knew it when I held thee close
But I could not capture thee
Freedom is thy definition

Last night she visited me
But now, she only exists
In the Realm Where Nothing is Real
Always the same dream
I want it so badly, it hurts
To make the fire burn again
So passionately and uncontrollably
Till there is no distance between
Where she ends and I begin
Simply living for her sake
Extreme pleasure and pain
And the inevitable feeling
That this is too good to last

The Eroticism of Death (3 sonnets)

Thou com'st to me at last
The one who knows no time
My life on Earth has passed
To stay would be a crime
You are the one, I know
Will take me far away
When you say, time to go
Then it will be okay
It's then I will discover
What's on the other side
You're like some secret lover
From whom I've tried to hide
But now I wait for you
And what you're here to do

I'm not afraid to leave
I'll take hold of your hand
There isn't time to grieve
Soon, I will understand
I'm waiting for your touch
Just like a lover who
Expecting oh so much
Will finally know it's true
You fill up all my senses
Come, fall on me like rain
I've let down my defenses
Abandoned all restrain
I can't resist your thrill
Do with me what you will

Then, take me to your home
And have my body too
You now are free to roam
Do what you need to do
I don't deny there's pleasure

In th' freedom that I crave
There is no greater treasure
Than that beyond the grave
I'll look into your eyes
As I breathe my last breath
Expire in your arms
And die the sweetest death
Then just one kiss from you
Is all you need to do

Part V

The Countdown

A Tale of Woe

Mine is a tale of woe
These are the things I know
Things that will break your heart
Always seem great, at the start
Loving somebody new
All of the things you do

Heaven on Earth, you say
You'll pay the price someday
Just when you learn to trust
People will do what they must
They lie and cheat and steal
Nobody's ever real

You can say what you will
Life, it goes on, but still
Everyone plays a game
Aren't we all the same?
Love, it will come and go
It's all the same, you know

Hurting more every day
Tell me another way
To find just what I need
People are full of greed
Nobody's got your back
You blink, then they attack

And if you need someone
Someday they will be done
Can't sleep at night, you see
Somebody rescue me
Mine is a tale of woe
These are the things I know

The Countdown

The countdown of my life begins
As yesteryear just fades away
And nothing's ever really clear
When I think of my life today

How many years do I have left
I wonder in my brain sometimes
So much remains for me to do
Until the bell, for me it chimes

Will I accomplish anything
That really makes my life complete
Or will my sins remain the same
Which I am destined to repeat

I have no knowledge to impart
To those who will require proof
My understanding is my own
To those to whom I seem aloof

I realize my time is short
Since I have lived so many years
I've seen so many come and go
That I have cried a thousand tears

Can this be true, it's almost gone
This life that I have known so well
An ending that is soon to come
Is all that I have left to tell

Sometimes I dream of days gone by
And people who I loved back then
They're only visions in my mind
But I can still remember when

I couldn't wait to start the day
The joy of living was so strong
I guess I really was a fool
Or maybe I was only wrong

I see the world with different eyes
The words are bitter on my tongue
To say all things are possible
When you are healthy and are young

The Prodical Son will return
Without the riches he once had
And hopes his father takes him back
Forgiving him for being bad

So don't wait till your time runs out
The countdown it begins today
Until the last day of your life
When every second ticks away

It Comes Back to You

Think about it
Close your eyes
Search your soul
If you remember it
It means something

The world goes on
Even after your troubles
Seem to take over
Till there's nothing left
But misery and pain

It's your decision
Try or give up
Take control of your life
And persevere

Try everything
Have no regrets
If you forget how
Concentrate harder
And you're no longer lost
Because eventually
It comes back to you

Desolation of the Soul

With a cold heart
And a love that has died
I will live my life
With nothing but the past
The future has no promise
I will breathe my last breath
And my eyes will close
Forever will not hold
Any meaning for me
I have done this thing
To never look back
Without any purpose
Nothing to cheer for
Try to let it go
And sleep in sorrow
My feelings non-existant
A soul without peace
None shall know me
Except through my songs
And sadness is my legacy
Alone within myself
To walk in sleep
A magnificent emptiness

Cause for Alarm

If you fear someday that you'll come to harm
You'll be assured, there's no cause for alarm
Watching the craziness that's on T.V.
Just don't believe everything that you see
All of the mayhem that's before your eyes
I'm sure it's not coming as a surprise

Ask the Authorities about their role
They'll say things clearly are under control
Sometimes I feel like I can't go outside
Then I don't think I'm safe where I reside
Now they can track you through your own cell phone
Why is it that they can't leave me alone

Just go to Facebook and you'll find a place
Nobody cares about personal space
You can find anyone in seconds flat
Complete with pictures of them and their cat
Big Brother's watching you every day
None of it's legal, but they find a way

Having your privacy now is a joke
It's not a problem for regular folk
Wanting to share things with everyone who
Feels exactly the same way that they do
Have you been hiding there, under a rock
While we all do this stuff around the clock

Sharing our photographs, stories and life
About our kids and our friends and our wife
More information than you'll ever need
We have connected the whole world indeed
What of this power that we give away
We're just not sure of the price that we'll pay

Let's say you wanted to just disappear
That's quite impossible, isn't it clear
Some kind of sinister plot has occured
When the lines we shouldn't cross, become blurred
If you fear someday that you'll come to harm
You'll be assured, there's no cause for alarm

Depression

You don't see it coming
Till you feel it arrive
The folks who can deal
Are the ones who survive
It's weight is so heavy
It crushes your soul
Emotions you're feeling
You just can't control

And if you give in
It can make you cry
When you notice your life
Is passing you by
It's filled with regrets
With sorrow and pain
When you think it's gone
It comes back again

And yes, I can feel it
When I am alone
The way it controls me
I weep and I moan
So I take a shower
To wash away things
That feed my depression
And all that it brings

Symbolism

In everything, I see
Something that isn't there
It's very plain to me
That no one seems to care

About what it all means
It's right before their eyes
But only can be seen
By one who really tries

And as the flowers die
A reason why they live
Their beauty there to see
What happiness they give

The seasons come and go
And so our lives, I guess
We never really know
Just why we're in this mess

Look further at the world
It spins around, you know
And we go for a ride
As we go to and fro

But what does it all mean
We want to understand
And on the other side
The Music plays the band

So look for symbolism
It's meaning will be clear
Then you will understand
The reason why we're here

The Words of the Dead

They've been ever sought after
What we hoped would be true
That from those who have died
We could know what to do
It's a tale of some quiet
Just as one lying still
To proceed without fear
And of your own free will

If there is one purpose
That their words do convey
Sometimes we need to worry
About only today
When we look to the future
Sometimes there isn't one
So then your final day
Will be when it's begun

You can relive your life
In a second or two
When it comes time to die
Will you know what to do
We believe what will happen
By the stories we hear
But when your life is done
Will things be as we fear

So we look to the Dead
To have something to say
But their words are not clear
Because that is their way
If they tell you their story
Do you think you won't die
All their troubles are over
There's no reason to lie

We imagine their words
Will be wise and be true
But they really don't change
What will happen to you
And suppose they could tell
Everything that you seek
Will that make you more strong
Or a little more weak

Since the first words were read
About those who have died
No one has found the truth
Though so many have tried
We all have in common
That which need not be said
When our time here is done
Then we all end up dead

Time Ticks Away

Time ticks away
Until you die
And you won't get
Another try

To live again
It's what you dread
There's no time left
And then you're dead

I often think
If I could see
How much more time
There is for me

Would I do things
So differently
And change my life
So drastically

And half a century
Is gone
Time to reflect
On what I've done

And is the world
A better place
Well, soon enough
I'll have to face

The One, I'm told
Will answer me
The reason why
We are to be

To love each other
As He did
Or am I acting
Like a kid

Do we create
Our destiny
I'm sure someday
That I will see

And yet I'm scared
To know my fate
I wonder if
It is too late

To change my life
If not today
I never will
Time ticks away

What Finer Fate Than Death

What finer fate than Death
It's beauty calls to me
Where everything is Truth
In all that we will be
There is no use in riches
Nor talent that we need
No one is ever hungry
There is an end to greed

Then truly are we perfect
The end of all our sin
Quite pointless to be jealous
There is nothing to win
We all become as brothers
When joined in endless sleep
All that is of this world
We do not get to keep

Our lives become as Legend
By others who would tell
Just how we were outstanding
To those who knew us well
We do not get to choose
When it's our time to go
But how we live our lives
Is for us all to know

Then die on your own terms
And live the way you should
Be kind and always selfless
Like you wish others would
Then when The Reaper comes
You won't be scared to go
When falls the Final Curtain
Hope you enjoyed the show

Unfinished

I look around
At what I see
And think about
How it could be

So many things
Have gone so well
But other stuff
Has gone to Hell

I need some magic
To command
So I can make
You understand

And here another
Day goes by
I'm closer to
My time to die

I'm almost ready
To give in
Is it too late
Can I begin

To reach my goal
Of what I'll be
My life goes on
Why can't I see

What lies ahead
I live in fear
And feel like now
The end is near

Then when I die
Will they all say
That he was nice
But lost his way
Potential he
Did not fulfill
It was a shame
But that was "Will"

And he got closer
Every day
But never could
Avoid delay

As for distractions
There were some
He thought his chance
Would never come

And so he never
Followed through
He left his life
Unfinished too

The Last Day of the Year

As if it were the last day of my life. I'm running out of ideas. Nothing to do or say any more. If anything can make it right; it eludes me. I'm completely lost. I can never start over again. I am a prisoner in my own life.

What horror!

Another year has gone by. But I am further away from God. I have lost all my self respect. Nobody knows how I suffer. Nobody cares.

What apathy!

Can't I just start over at day one? There are 365 days in a year. It can only be the first day once. So many days, into so many months and so many years.

What brevity!

Since I have no trust in the world, I look for the meaning of life. Of course, it cannot be found. Nobody knows where to look. (If it had teeth, it would have bitten you...)

What surprise!

I go slowly, I go quickly. I'm alive and then, no longer. These days fill me with anxiety. And I wonder how much time I have left. Is there any happiness left for me?

What carelessness!

Those I thought I loved, only linger in my dreams. I go back in time to a place that never was. Would I have ever left, had I known that my fate would always remain as it is?

What irony!

All the joy that I had is dead. My heart is no longer living. I look forward to the end of it all. And I'm scared it won't come soon enough.

What despair!

Going to the Graveyard

Going to the graveyard soon
To retrieve my wounded soul
So I'll be a little closer
To achieve my final goal

Where it doesn't look suspicious
For a lonely man to cry
Because everyone is sad
And they know the reason why

Here my solitude's accepted
If by chance, that I am seen
It's a place to cry in private
And a place we all have been

Where my heart is slowly dying
I try not to lose my trust
Here I will be all alone
When I do just what I must

It seems things are always clearer
When I come into this place
Where things are all in perspective
As I linger in its space

And the pain that I am feeling
Well, it hardly can compare
To the questions of existence
I will ponder if I dare

Regrets

Total sadness is my fate
Can my life change, is it too late
Then sooner dead because of fear
It is for this, I shed a tear
So complicated, every day
Impossible to find a way
To just go back and start again
I'd go right now, just tell me when

And live those days, with no mistakes
Discover when my heart awakes
It tells me what is meant to be
And all the things I didn't see
Come rescue me from all my sins
Take me back to where it begins
I was good once, but now I'm not
Remind me of what I've forgot

And then tell me, who did I kill
The blood remains on my hands still
Who have I wronged, who hates me now
Tell me it will work out, somehow
And Karma is as Karma does
I can't remember how it was
The eyes I had once, now are blind
The things I did, that weren't kind

I feel them more as I grow old
The things that I have never told
I swore that I would never tell
And that will send my soul to Hell
I can't escape my Judgment Day
When for my sins, I'll surely pay
The life I've lived in selfishness
Will damn me then, or so I'd guess

Was I that boy, so pure of heart
Before the fall, when did I start
To lose my way, towards God's own plan
Becoming just a selfish man
Who does what's best for his own good
And never doing what he should
You die one day and that is that
It isn't good to be so fat

Where everything is easy, too
It isn't what is good for you
The struggle makes you stronger still
To do things of your own free will
When it's not easy, then you'll see
That this is how your life should be
The work you put in, you'll get out
To figure out what life's about

It's not all you, there's others who
Depend upon the things you do
We're all connected in some way
So do your best, that's all I'll say
Then live your life with no regrets
And be the one who just forgets
What others do, you can forgive
It is the best way you can live

I'll tell you when my time is through
That I'll do this, if you will too
And when we go, we'll be at peace
To finally have found some release
So don't give up, it's not too late
Don't let despondence be your fate
Encouragement, I'll give to you
And that is all I'll ask of you

If I Die Tonight

If I were to die tonight
I would be content
Knowing everything I know
Exactly what it's meant

I have lived a life complete
Sometimes gone astray
Seems like any moment it
All could end today

Others die and others live
Lives without a clue
Never know the reasons why
They do what they do

There has always been some cause
Why I've lived this way
Other people just don't know
They live day to day

Those who don't have love to give
Fade away somehow
Others keep it to themselves
I say, give it now

Someday we won't be around
When our lives are done
Just give over what you have
One day you'll be gone

I hope that we all can have
Lives that we dream of
Then our hearts will be at peace
And be filled with love

The Invisible

You only have to imagine them
The things we cannot see
But we know, do exist
You can feel their reality
If only in the intangible realm
That is inside your mind

Beauty is such a thing
That you see in real life
But feel in your soul even more
It helps you to create things
They reflect the light that shines
From deep within you

It is truly where love exists
Although it is invisible to the eye
You know that it is real
Can we ever know for certain
What we believe is what is true
Maybe yes, Maybe no

But these are the things
That are unmistakably tied
To the core of our humanity
And are very much the reason
That we exist at all

So try not to overlook them
Or you may just miss
What it is that you do not see
But is most important to us
As creatures of the world

For to truly cherish them
Is to be in touch with the universe
As it is and as it should be
A reflection of our own selves
That we would be sure to miss
If we are not careful to
See that which cannot be seen

I Don't Know Why

I don't know why
Sometimes I cry
I just get sad
Is that so bad?
I know it's true
So how 'bout you
There is no shame
To feel the same

I watch T.V.
Sometimes I see
Things late at night
That aren't right
Love stories too
Can make me blue
When girl meets boy
It's such a joy

That I can't stop
The tears that drop
Down from my face
It's a disgrace
There is no fear
To shed a tear
When it's just me
No one can see

I let them flow
No one will know
They pour like rain
It's just insane
I let them fly
Don't even try
To keep control
It's in my soul

And is it true
You do it too
Sometimes we just
Do what we must
This poem may seem
Like some strange dream
I will not lie
I don't know why

It Takes a Long Time

It takes a long time
To recover your soul
And it never is easy
If that is your goal

But if you try your hardest
You'll see it can be done
You must go to the place
Where your life had begun

To the days you were younger
And your heart, it was strong
Then you'll soon realize
It is where you belong

And if you have the words
You can then make them rhyme
But you must keep in mind that
It takes a long time

I Become Like Starlight

As the words leave my mind
Become one with the page
Seems to me that I find
That along with my age
That Time's ticking away
Towards my very last day

All the thoughts I posess
That were once only mine
I have come to confess
Write them down, line by line
So that they become verse
Some for best, some for worse

I decide what I'll say
Then I let the words flow
Till they find their own way
And know which way to go
Then they find their way home
Become born as a poem

When I ponder my fate
As my life seems to fade
Those things that I create
Will help me to evade
Passing into the night
Without shining a light

The Day You Left

The day you left
I woke up late
But your last hour
Wouldn't wait
Discovered that
You went away
Black Friday was
Your final day

The day you left
I didn't cry
I felt like this
Was not goodbye
Somehow, I thought
It wasn't real
Confused by how
It made me feel

The day you left
I got the call
And didn't understand
It all
I heard that you
Had fell asleep
But did not know
You fell so deep

The day you left
I thought of you
And everything
That we'd been through
That since I was
A little boy
You always gave
Me so much joy

The day you left
I knew I'd miss
The love within
A mother's kiss
Never again
To feel the touch
Of someone who
Loved me that much

Made in the USA
Middletown, DE
27 February 2017